PRAISE FOR THE BASIC WILDLIFE REHABILITATION SERIES

"These are responsible, instructional handbooks for wildlife care in the immediate stabilization of rescued wildlife, emergency first aid treatment, appropriate food, habitat design, and basic rehabilitation and release techniques."

—Richard A. Alter, D.V.M.

"Informative and to the point...ethical...wonderful job illustrating...I would recommend the series as a good introduction to rehabilitation...well-organized, quick to look through."

—Gail Buhl, wildlife biologist,
NWRA Quarterly, 1996

ENDORSEMENTS

"The FIRST AID FOR WILDLIFE section is full of essential, practical information, especially in the area of immediate first aid."

—Laura Simon, president,
Connecticut Wildlife Rehabilitation Association

"This book is for anyone who loves and cares about wildlife. It provides basic techniques in rescue, diet and housing, resources, do's and don'ts about when to help, when not, and how."

—Cathy Zamecnik, founder
and director, Little Feet

"This basic manual will help distressed wildlife in the first emergency stages and answer those first questions about shock and dehydration, diseases, wounds, fractures, general rehabilitation and release, what to do and who to call."

—Hope M. Douglas, founder and
director, Wind Over Wings

I Found A Baby Duck, What Do I Do?

I Found A Baby Duck, What Do I Do?

Dale Carlson
Illustrated by Hope M. Douglas, M.A.

BOOK FAITH INDIA
Delhi

I Found A Baby Duck, What Do I Do?

Published by
BOOK FAITH INDIA
414-416 Express Tower
Azadpur Commercial Complex
Delhi, India 110033
Tel. [91-11] 713-2459. Fax [91-11] 724-9674
E-mail: pilgrim@del2.vsnl.net.in

Distributed by
PILGRIMS BOOK HOUSE
P.O.Box 3872
Kathmandu, Nepal
Tel. [977-1] 424942. Fax [977-1] 424943.
E-mail: pilgrims@wlink.com.np
WebSite: www.pilgrimsbooks.com

Varanasi Branch
PILGRIMS BOOK HOUSE
B 27/98-A-8, Durga Kund
Varanasi, India 221001
Tel. [91-542] 314060. Fax [91-542] 314059, 312788
E-mail: pilgrim@lw1.vsnl.net.in

Cover design by Dr. Sasya

First Book Faith India Edition. : 2000
Printed with permission from Bick Publishing House, Madison, CT.

ISBN 81-7303-209-2

The contents of this book may not be reproduced, stored or copied in any form—printed, electronic, photocopied or otherwise—except for excerpts used in review, without the written permission of the publisher.

Printed in India

INTRODUCTION

This is not just a book about animals. This is a book about when and how to rescue creatures in distress; basic physical examination for injury; first aid; species and age identification; diets and feeding techniques; basic housing; and general rehabilitation and release techniques. This book will not teach you to be a veterinarian or a wildlife rehabilitator, but it will teach you initially how to help distressed, injured, and orphaned animals, and who to call for professional help.

Rehabilitation is to give back life. Young, orphaned mammals, nursing or newly weaned, have simple yet essential needs for clean, warm environments, specialized formula and diets, and nurturing, surrogate parenting from human caregivers. It is necessary to have a kind heart, but it is equally necessary to know when to leave a mammal nest alone, or a fledgling bird learning to fly, how to rescue properly, examine, feed, house, rehabilitate, and release appropriately.

Rehabilitation is to give back life. The experience of saving life changes people as well as ensures a healthy future for our environment. People ask, why bother to save one small bird or squirrel? A rehabilitator's answer is that we save life because it needs saving, and because it is becoming evident that everything in the universe is connected to everything else, and so everything, no matter how small, matters. A raccoon or opossum has the same life force flowing its small body as we do. When you care for any single creature, you care for all life. Many of the species on our planet are dying out, and if too many of them die, we will die also.

To save a species, you have to save its young. Independent, backyard rehabilitators, many of whom are young people, save wildlife by the thousands and release them back into the wild. Rehabilitators do not take prisoners, but restore and release. They take no pets for their own sakes, but restore and release back to the wild when possible. No matter how attached one gets to orphaned or injured wildlife, to rehabilitate is to raise, nurture, teach, and release. It is also up to us to educate, to teach that whether animals are hurt by nature, deliberate hurting (as if killing for fun were a fully human trait, or it were sporting to kill a defenseless animal), or because we have inadvertently invaded their habitat, it is up to us to help.

Rehabilitators also understand the limits of rehabilitation. Any sick or injured adult, or infant or juvenile, needs to be taken to a veterinarian unless you have the necessary skills.

We can all learn to rehabilitate. Even though helping hurt and distressed animals seems like an easy thing to do, it isn't always as simple as it looks.

Your state, like most states, may require a legal permit to raise and release wildlife, and for most permits, training is required. Call your Department of Environmental Protection (or whatever your state calls its department of conservation) or your Federal Fish and Wildlife Department for advice, for the telephone number of your nearest local rehabilitator, for information on how you can get training and your own permit.

REMEMBER: These skills are for adult use only. Young children should not handle wildlife for their own safety, and the well-being of the animal. It is important for parents, teachers, librarians, and wildlife professionals to teach children how to respect and rehabilitate wildlife. But it is equally important, for the safety, from injury and disease, of both children and wildlife, that only adults handle orphaned and injured animals. Help them to respect and observe what you are doing, but it can be dangerous for children to handle wildlife, and even more dangerous for infant wildlife to be handled by inexperienced hands.

CONTENTS

1. RESCUE

2. IDENTIFICATION AND STAGES OF GROWTH

3. BASIC DIET

4. HOUSING

5. RELEASE

6. TIPS

APPENDIX: Reference Books
Recommended Manuals
Initial Care and First Aid Supplies

RESCUE

Why Birds Get Hurt

You can come upon hurt and helpless birds in all sorts of places for all sorts of reasons. They can fall or be pushed out of nests in traps. They can get stunned by cars, by flying into big glass windows, or high wires. People shoot and wound them. They get caught in boat propellers, or plastic bags and can connectors. They are killed and sickened by our oil spills, poisoned by our pesticides and toxic wastes. They are hurt not only by our ways of living, but by our domestic pets, cats in particular, and even more by our unwitting invasion into and destruction of their natural habitat.

Sometimes they get hurt by weather or in nature. Orphaned and injured birds are found in cities and in the country, in forests, on beaches, in deserts, by streams and lakes. But whether it is our fault or nature's fault, we need to save life simply because it needs saving.

1
RESCUE

Why Birds Get Hurt

You can come upon hurt and helpless birds in all sorts of places for all sorts of reasons. They can fall or be pushed out of nests in trees. They can get stunned by cars, by flying into big glass windows, or high wires. People shoot and wound them. They get caught in boat propellers, or plastic bags and can connectors. They are killed and sickened by our oil spills, poisoned by our pesticides and toxic wastes. They are hurt not only by our ways of living, but by our domestic pets, cats in particular, and even more by our unwitting invasion into and destruction of their natural habitat.

Sometimes they get hurt by each other or in nature. Orphaned and injured birds are found in towns and in the country, in forests, on beaches, by highways and lakes. But whether it is our fault or nature's fault, people who care save life simply because it needs saving.

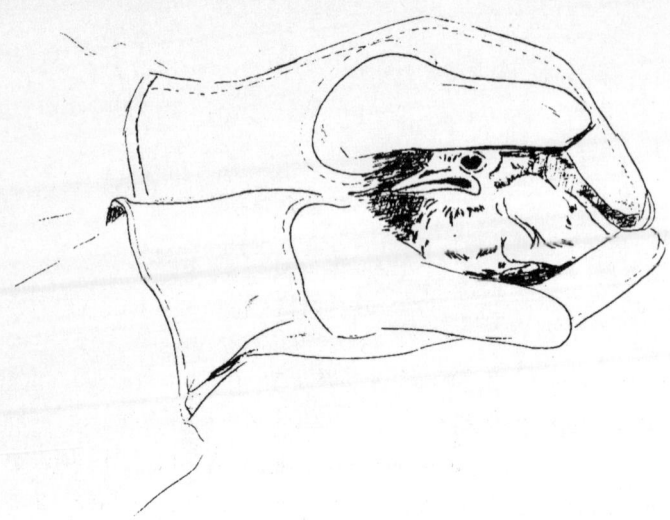

Watch, Wait, Warm

These are the key words in rescuing wildlife in distress. The first instinct in people who care is to rush in and save. The trouble with too much haste is that without proper observation and information, you may be kidnapping a bird in no need of rescue.

Watch first for an hour or so unless you see blood or an open wound; or a leg, beak, or wing damaged; or that the bird is cat-caught or unconscious. A fledgling or nestling may simply have been coaxed from the nest to teach it to fly. Often the parents have gone for food.

Wait until you are sure the baby is abandoned. Safety for the bird means determining its age, size, and condition. Safety for you means not handling a bird too large for you, or any raptors such as hawks and eagles, by yourself. Call for professional help if you cannot easily hold a distressed bird in your hands. A small bird pecks a little. The claws and beaks of larger birds can be dangerous.

Warm the bird. Make a nest of your hands. Cup the bird to keep it warm, quiet, and in restful darkness. It will be shocked and scared from its fall or accident. Don't be frightened. Now, carry the bird gently in your hands. You will need the help of a licensed rehabilitator to care for the lost baby, even if this is only over the telephone. This is true even more if the bird is hurt.

When your bird is warm, and you find it is unhurt, put it back in its nest if you can. Or make a nest out of a hanging box or planter filled with leaves and hang it near the spot you found the baby. Watch again to see if its mother or father comes back. Most birds have little sense of smell. You can handle baby birds. Parents will not reject them.

It is always a good idea to wear gloves when you pick up birds or any kind of wildlife. Proceed gently but firmly and quietly. Birds stress easily.

If no parent comes after an hour or two, or if the bird is hurt, the situation is now up to you.

DO continue to keep the bird warm.

DO NOT feed it food or water right away.

Initial Care

Place the bird in a warm, quiet, semi-dark place. You will need two boxes: a small one for a nest, and a larger one to put the nest inside of.

Make a tiny nest box. A berry box filled with scrunched up toilet paper is perfect. It is important to support a baby bird's body so the bones will grow right.

A cardboard box will do for the larger container. An aquarium tank with wire mesh cover is fine. Line it with paper toweling, an old T-shirt, a piece of sheet. No newspapers for babies, and never colored papers (color is poison).

Put the baby inside the nest and the nest inside the bigger box. Continue to provide warmth with a 60 watt bulb adjusted at 12" to 18" above the nest box. At night, use a 60 watt blue

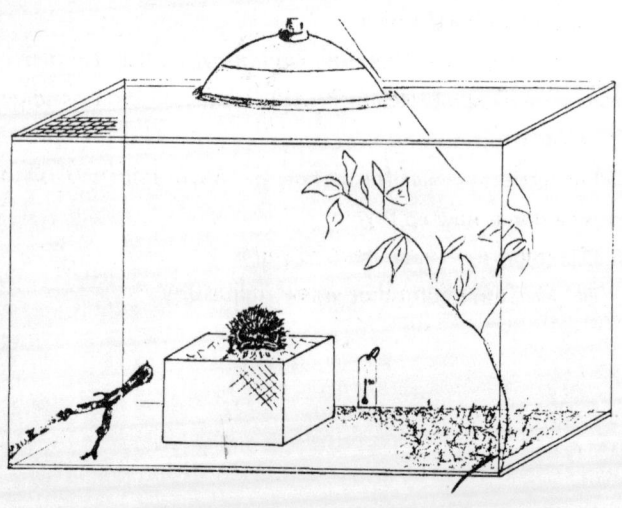

bulb or your bird will be unable to sleep. Do not use Teflon-coated bulbs, as these give off toxic fumes.

Watch now, don't handle. Small birds suffer stress from handling.

First Aid

For first aid techniques, use volume seven of this series. Most immediately, look to see if a wing droops. Look to see if it can't stand on one of its legs. Look to see if there is any bleeding. Watch to see if the bird just lies on its side or breathes through its open bill. You will need help to treat any injury or disease. Call for advice. Call a trained animal rehabilitator if you know

Call for help if you cannot easily hold a bird in your hands.

one. If not, call your Department of Environmental Protection, or your vet or local police, who will have telephone numbers for a wildlife rehabilitator near you.

REMEMBER:

- DO NOT feed it immediately. Any bird, a baby or adult bird, may eat too much too fast if it's too hungry and go into shock.

- DO NOT OFFER LIQUID. If you offer a drink, even by dropper or in a little shallow bowl, to a baby bird, you risk drowning it by getting fluids into its breathing hole.

- DO GIVE it bits of watermelon, berries, or grape halves to rehydrate, restore body fluids and nourish. Some birds gape naturally. Some beaks you must pry open gently.

2
IDENTIFICATION AND STAGES OF GROWTH

While your critter is resting and recovering from the shock of its accident or abandonment and rescue, it is a good time for you to identify and learn about what you've got. When you find a baby bird, or one is brought to you, be sure to take notes. Record all pertinent information concerning the bird: where it was found, habitat, tree, or ground; its size and coloration; circumstances such as presence of adult bird screaming or divebombing the rescuer. This information will guide you as to species, and especially important, diet. Birds need the correct food, or they will die, even if they eat what you give them and seem full.

Do not overhandle (birds have higher blood pressure than mammals and extreme fright may cause the aorta to rupture and the bird to die). But look carefully. Size, colors, habitat will give you clues as to the species. Check a really good field guide bird book at your public library, if you don't own one. There are many more species of birds than mammals, some 8,900 in the world, over 800 in North America alone. Birds are designed on the principle of being strong but lightweight. Their skeletal structure consists of hollow bones that provide a strong but light frame.

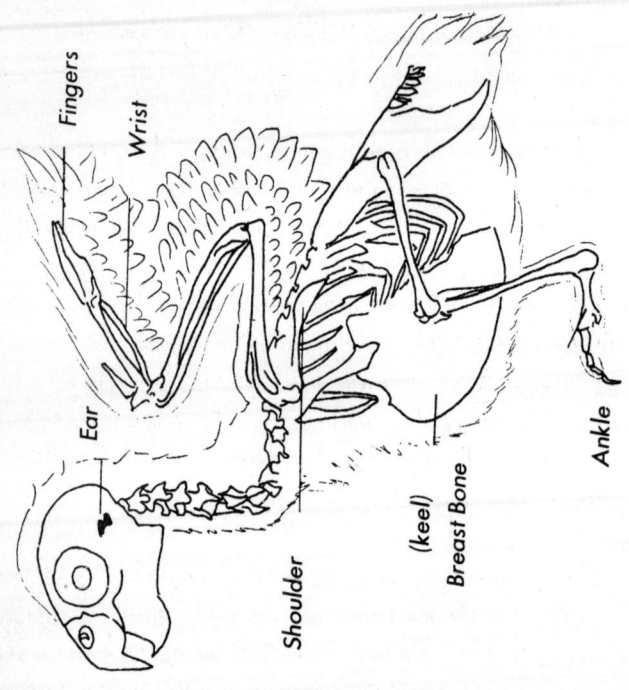

Their limbs are paired: the forelimbs are wings for flying; the hindlimbs adapted for various functions such as perching, wading, grasping, climbing, etc. Their young are divided into four categories:

1. **precocial chicks :** born with eyes open, down-covered, leave nest within one to two days after hatching, either completely independent or follow parents but find own food like ducks, shorebirds, or are given food (grebes) or shown food (quail)

2. **semi-precocial:** born with eyes open, down-covered, stay in nest, like gulls

3. **semi-altricial :** born with down, but unable to leave nest, some eyes open like herons and hawks, some eyes closed like owls

4. **altricial:** eyes closed, little or no down, unable to leave nest—this includes passerines— songbirds

It is their ability to fly that has given birds a range of habitat greater than mammals. It is their variety that can be confusing. Species, as well as age, is fundamentally important to diet and manner of feeding, and also information as to day or night activity, whether migratory or living in one place year round. These facts are vital to healthy rearing.

Rehabilitators generally divide birds into four groups: songbirds with various diets; shorebirds/waterfowl which eat fish (herons), rodents (loons), cereal grains (swans, ducks, geese);

raptors which eat rodents and other small prey; game birds (heavy-bodied, largely terrestrial birds such as grouse, pheasant, quail) which eat grain mixtures. There are also special pellet diets for certain waterfowl, and unmedicated poultry mashes, frozen mice or rats (supplemented), and commercial bird-of-prey diets, though the last are still controversial. Check the appendices of this book for organizations and reading material to find additional information for the diets of shorebirds/waterfowl, raptors, and gamebirds, or call a rehabilitator or the organizations listed.

This book is primarily concerned with caring for small birds. Here is a page of some common songbirds divided into feeding types.

1. Aerial-feeding insect-eaters (swallows, swifts)

2. Foliage-feeding insect-eaters (chickadees, wrens, wood-peckers)

3. Ground-feeding insect-eaters (robins, sparrows)

4. Seed-eaters (finches)

5. Omnivores who eat everything (crows, blue jays, starlings, mocking birds)

6. Columbids (rock doves or pigeons and mourning doves)

House Sparrow	Hairy Woodpecker
Barn Swallow	Nuthatch
Starling	Morning Dove

AGES AND STAGES

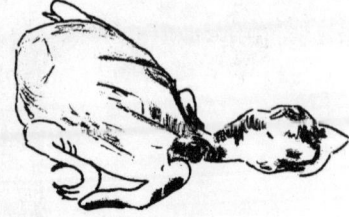

HATCHLING: eyes closed, no feathers: week one

NESTLING: eyes open, hopping, beginning feathers: week 2-3

FLEDGLING: feathered and flying but not self feeding: 25-28 days

Along with species, you need to find out your bird's age. Here is a page of birds at different ages and stages of development.

HATCHLING: eyes closed, no feathers: week one

NESTLING: eyes open, hopping, beginning feathers: week 2-3

FLEDGLING: feathered and flying but not self-feeding: 25-28 days

Not only do different kinds of birds eat different food, birds of different ages eat different food. Only the right food at the right time will help birds to thrive.

A NOTE TO BIRD-LOVERS: Do not feed bread to wild birds, songbirds or waterfowl, or shore or game birds. Bread fills them with empty calories and may cause rickets, airplane wing, and other debilitating deformities. A pocketful or bag full of cracked corn is perfect!

And if you're going to fill bird-feeders—do so year round. Don't get wild birds to depend on a food source, build nests for their babies, and suddenly cut them off. And please, bell—preferably house—your cats if you are going to feed birds near your home.

AGES AND STAGES

HATCHLING: eyes closed, no feathers; week one

NESTLING: eyes open, hopping, beginning feathers; week 2-3

FLEDGLING: feathered and flying but not self feeding; 25-28 days

3
BASIC DIET

Baby Bird Checklist

1. You have got your bird warm, rested, and calm.

2. You have seen it is not too hurt or stressed.

3. You have given it rehydrating fruit.

4. You have identified your bird and its age in your book.

Where is she?

Feed Your Bird

You have waited for twenty or thirty minutes to allow the bird to rest and recover and warm, and by now it may be looking or sounding or acting really hungry. It may be gaping (opening its mouth) or peeping (calling) for food.

Emergency Food

You can feed in tiny bits:

1. dry (complete) dog or cat food soaked in a little warm water
2. mushy canned dog or cat food or strained baby beef

Formula for a Baby, Hatchling or Nestling

1/2 cup complete canned dog food or strained baby beef
2 Tablespoons high protein baby cereal
1 hard-boiled egg yolk (3 yolks=1/4 cup) crumbled
moisten with warm water or fruit juice, not milk.

For a 1-4 day old nestling add enough liquid (water or fruit juice) to make a slurry that can be fed with a syringe. For older nestlings add enough liquid to make the mixture the consistency of canned dog food.

Commercial nestling diets are available, including Lafeber's NUTRI-START, Wild Wings PASSERINE DIETS. Use these diets according to instructions.

Adult Bird Diets

Food for your bird as it gets bigger, both fledgling and adult:

1 part canned dog food, or dog chow soaked in water
1 part high protein baby cereal with wheat germ
applesauce
Make a mush of all these ingredients

Feeding wild birds in captivity is a technique that takes training and skill, as well as a knowledge of species-specific diets. There are manuals listed in the appendices that suggested appropriate diets for all categories of wild birds, but unless you are licensed it is not legal for you to keep the birds. Call for professional help.

Proper finger-feeding technique

How Often To Feed

Baby birds have to eat very often. You will need to feed as often as they need to eat, just the way a mother or father bird does. For baby birds, the general rule is every 20-30 minutes from 7 a.m. to 7 p.m. At 10-14 days old, feed every hour. At 15 days to fledgling, feed every 2 hours.

Amounts To Feed

HATCHLING	100% of body weight per day
FLEDGLING	50% of body weight per day
ADULT	feed only morning and evening 25% of body weight per day

When feeding nestlings, avoid over-filling crop so that it is never hard to the touch.

Droppings

Defecation usually follows feeding. Healthy droppings are firm, usually forest green and white for most birds. Songbird droppings are usually brown, but reflect whatever has been eaten, as in berry diets produce purple or red droppings. Our suggested diet will produce brown in variable shades. Bright green or mustard yellow may indicate bacterial infection; diarrhea may be foul-smelling; black droppings or no droppings, digestion problems. Diet and constipation must be corrected immediately, or the bird may die in a short time.

Grit is required for the digestion of many seed and grain-eating birds such as doves, ducks, and geese. Feed grit (necessary for digestion) by sprinkling over food.

Feeding Techniques

For very young birds, use tip of your finger to offer the mush. You can also use a cotton swab without the cotton to push food into the gaping bill, past the glottis, into the throat. Do this very carefully so as not to injure the bird any further. Older birds will eat on their own.

Check Bird Diets

Brukner Nature Center, IWRC, NWRA, and others in the appendix will list diets based on sound nutrition for all species of birds and are periodically updated as needed. Consult your wildlife rehabilitator, and veterinarian, as well, for the special diets of waterfowl and shorebirds and diving birds that include fish; game birds that eat special grain mixtures such as layer pellets or mash, or even better gamebird crumbles; and raptors such as owls, hawks, and eagles who need rodents and other prey food.

There are two main types of small bird diets.

Grain-eaters will eat mixed bird seed.

Insect-eaters will need worms and insect foods. You can buy these dried at most pet stores. Or you can catch them yourself.

Many adult birds thrive on an easy combination of canned dog food, berries, grapes, veggies, sunflower seeds.

Clean the nest and box or cage every day.

Offer fresh food and shallow bowl of water every day. Most songbirds like to bathe every day, in water, sunshine, dust, or a combination of these.

4
HOUSING

First Home

You have already made a small nest from scrunched toilet paper in a berry box or similar container and placed it inside a bigger cardboard box or aquarium or cage. Your baby bird will be fine here as a hatchling, even a nestling.

As your bird grows into a fledgling, juvenile, and adult, in captivity a bird's housing requirements vary according to its size, species, and physical needs. Injured birds in particular need a quiet, private area. Birds recovering from injuries need room to strengthen damaged limbs. Fledglings need sizable flight habitats, plenty of room for preening, bathing, feeding, and flight practice.

Second Home

The International Wildlife Rehabilitation Council (IWRC) and the National Wildlife Rehabilitators Association (NWRA) have both standardized wild animal housing requirements as to species, size, anatomical differences and needs. Just as you would call these organizations for updated diets, you can call them for housing requirements.

To begin with, you will need to build or buy a cage with enough room for hopping. It must have mesh fine enough so your bird cannot fly out or any other animal get in. Fill the hopping cage with things from your bird's original natural environment. Use your field guide and your imagination. Make sure there are perches, branches, and twigs. Put a few dried leaves in the cage. Your bird will miss the woods or the marsh or the water's edge where it was born.

Please keep your cages clean of old food, feces, too much collected debris. You do not want sickness—or to attract predators by the smell. Most important is that cleanliness keeps diseases and parasites at bay and prevents bacteria and mold. Provide clean water daily for drinking and frequently for bathing so the bird can keep itself and its feathers in good shape.

Third Home

At the juvenile and certainly at the adult stage, a bird's specialized anatomy and needs must be taken into account. By now, you will certainly have contacted a professional or be in training for your own license. Special housing requirements must be understood.

You will need to build a flight cage, or aviary. Have it look like this.

It will have to be tall enough for your bird to fly up in. It will need a flight or nesting shelf for the night with an area of protection from the weather. It will need the right kind of nesting box.

Put in tall, thick, leafy branches to look like a tree, buy potted trees. Put in a food dish. Put in dirt dishes, plants. Put in a water and bath dish. Put thick leaves and pine needles on the floor. Use newspaper underneath for an indoor cage.

Make sure there are plenty of perches at different flight levels.

Do check up on special requirements. For instance: waterfowl need pools for swimming, diving, or wading, and padded floors to protect feet; hawks and owls need padded perches to protect their feet when perching; woodpeckers need vertical logs for climbing and drumming.

There is great pleasure in watching recovering and maturing birds learn to use their wings and develop their skills. Enjoy them. From hatchling to release is only a few weeks.

Companionship

Most birds are lonely by themselves like any other animal. If you can find a bird that is similar, that is the best. If not, certain species such as swans, geese, and other waterfowl can be housed together. So can many types of songbirds. Do watch, however, for personality and gender differences that may provoke attack or prevent proper feeding.

If all you have is the one baby bird, you will have to be its surrogate parent, teach it not only to eat and to fly, but the dangers of household pets and what else to be afraid of, humans in particular. You and your pets may not hurt the bird. Other pets, wild animals, and humans will.

Imprinting, attaching to its own species, is very important. If all your bird sees is you, it will be hard for it to learn to be a bird, to sing the right songs, to learn what to fear, to find food in the wild and mate and nest

HOPPING CAGE
(18" x 18" x 18")

Galvanized or Brass Screws

Hardware Cloth Outside

Avian Netting Inside

Dried Leaves

Nest Box

Wire

Avian Netting Inside

Hardware Cloth Outside

Solid Wood

8'

2'

2'

2'

10'

5'

Double Door

4'

FLIGHT CAGE for small birds view with one door. (see top view)

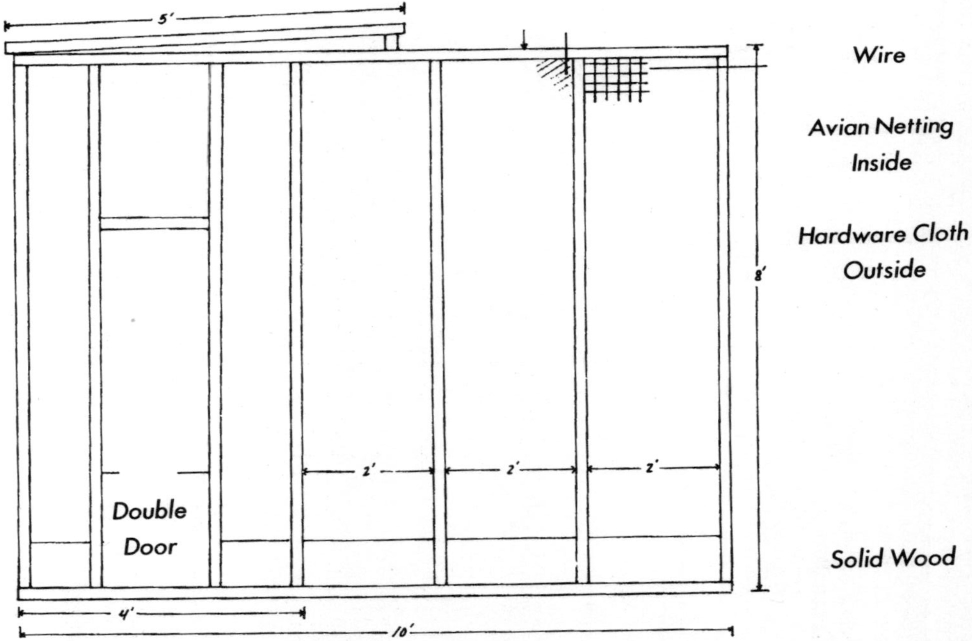

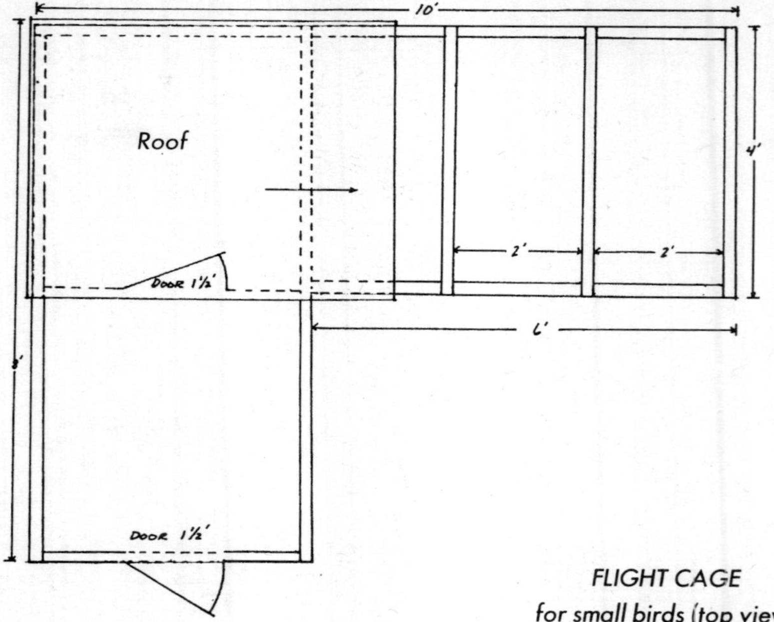

FLIGHT CAGE
for small birds (top view)

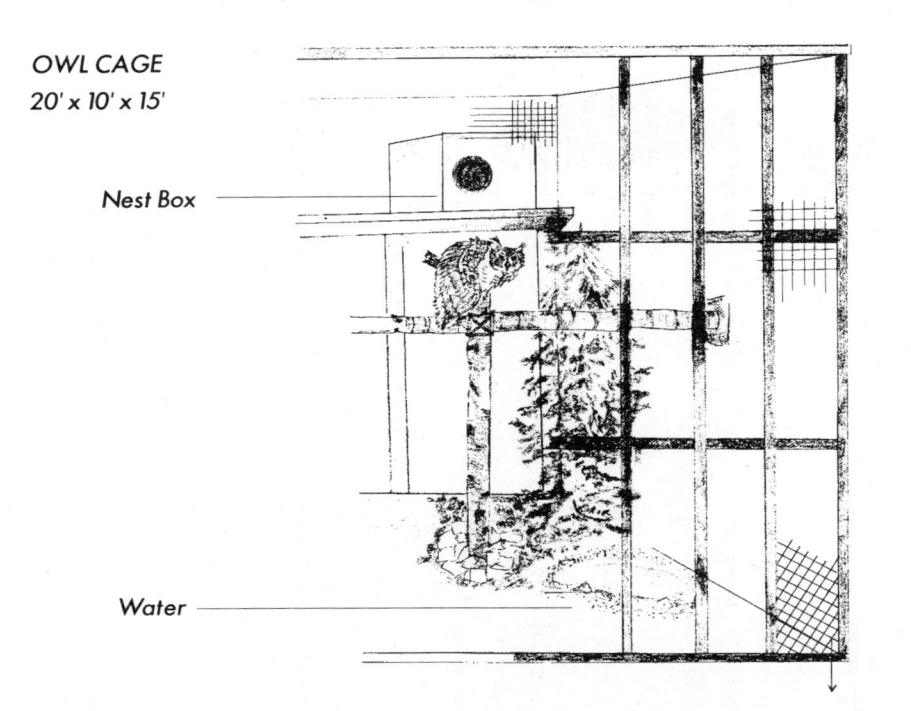

OWL CAGE
20' x 10' x 15'

Nest Box

Water

Avian Netting
Inside

Chain Link
Outside

Wire
Underground
18"

WATERFOWL/SHOREBIRD AVIARY
Night Enclosure, Design by L. Schimmel

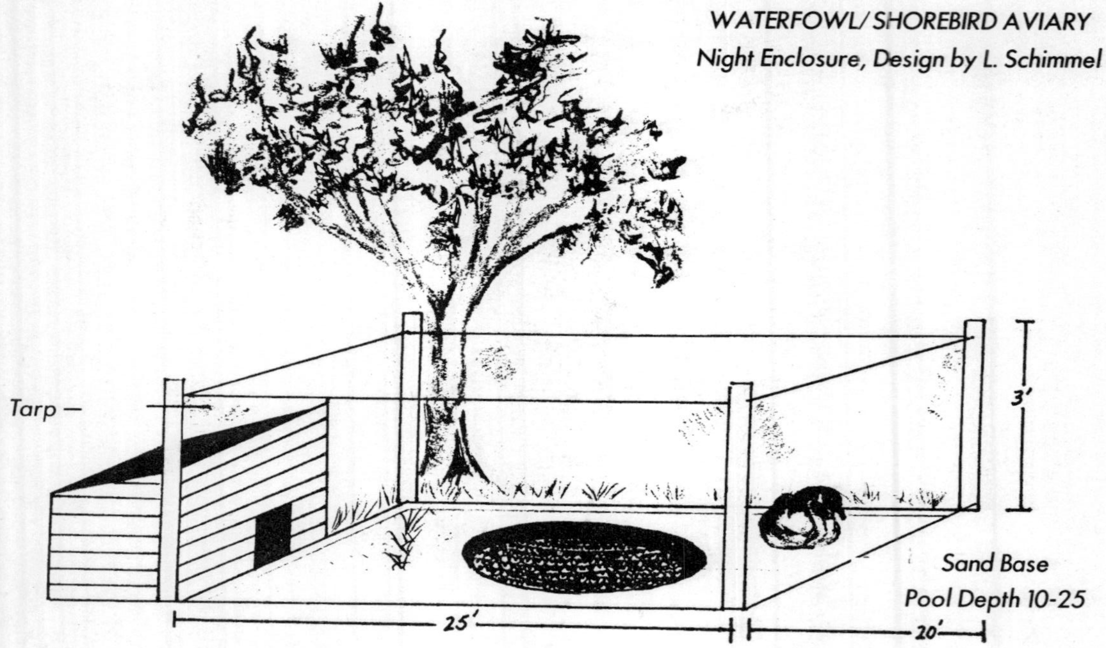

5
RELEASE

Your bird was born free. Rehabilitators do not make prisoners of healthy creatures but release them back into the wild. It is a good idea to check release sites, not only by reading about bird species in their natural habitats, but by talking to local natural resource officials, biologists, other rehabilitators. You will need to find out whether there are similar species in the area (for mating and company and to ensure there is the right kind of food) ; what the area's carrying capacity for the species is (too much competition for mating and feeding); whether there are too many people, roads and therefore cars and cats and dogs, in the area.

Let the bird live in an outdoor flight cage before you release it. Do this for one week before release.

If you live in a city or cannot leave it in an outside aviary, wait a little longer before releasing. After release, leave food out for the bird for a week or two. This will help it not to starve while it learns to find food on its own. After a while, it will no longer return. You will have done a successful release.

Release is the most important part of wildlife rehabilitation once you have saved a life. Wildlife is not ours to possess, only to help in its distress and let go.

It may help to remember the differences between domestic animals who have been bred to live with humans and changed genetically in the process like dogs and cats and cows, and those who have been wrongly imprinted (birds) or tamed or habituated like mammals. Captive animals are originally wild, caught animals whose original nature is unchanged, whose wildness is part of them. We are animals with feelings. So are they. No one wants to live life against its nature.

Sometimes a bird is too injured or too young to survive. Sometimes it cannot or will not thrive in captivity. More than most species, birds mask their pain to deter predators. But a bird may hurt too much and die to release itself. It is not your fault. You did your best. You protected its life and its dying, kept it fed, warmed, and safe from the fear of predators.

You cared.

Growing away is part of rehabilitating.

Grief over release and death is part of rehabilitating. We have discovered the best ways to handle grief is to talk about it with someone appropriate, and then go on to help the next bird.

6
TIPS

Hot Tips for You

1. Don't handle a bird if you don't want to.

2. Call for help and advice.

3. Don't birdnap a baby bird. Watch for parents before rescuing.

4. Your goal in rescuing a bird is its release when possible. No critter wants a life prison sentence unless it's too hurt to survive.

5. Wear heavy gloves for larger birds. They use beaks and claws under stress.

6. Keep any critter away from your face.

7. Wash hands first for bird's sake.

8. Wash hands after handling for your own sake.

Hot Tips for Critters

1. In the case of found babies, watch for parents first: DON'T BIRDNAP while parents are off to find food.

2. Warm bird first in your hands, or against your body.

3. Put in warm, quiet, dark place to recover from shock.

4. It is a good idea to give rehydration fruit before food.

5. Never feed a cold, starving bird before warming and rehydrating.

6. Keep household pets away, however gentle. Birds and other small wildlife need to learn to fear cats and dogs.

7. Call your Department of Environmental Protection or Conservation, or your local wildlife rehabilitator, for advice and help. Your veterinarian or your local police will have telephone numbers.

APPENDIX A

REFERENCE BOOKS

Audubon Handbooks, McGraw-Hill Book Company, New York, San Francisco, Singapore, Toronto, et al.

The Merck Veterinary Manual, Merck & Co., Inc., Rahway, New Jersey.

Peterson Field Guide Series, A Field Guide to the Mammals of North America, North of Mexico, A Field Guide to Birds (regional), by Roger Tory Peterson, Houghton, Mifflin Company, Boston.

Stokes Nature Guides, A Guide to Animal Tracking and Behavior, A Guide to Bird Behavior, Volume I, II, III, by Donald Stokes, Little, Brown and Company, Boston.

RECOMMENDED MANUALS

Basic Manual Wildlife Rehabilitation Series (7-VOL), Bick Publishing House, Madison, Connecticut. 203/245-0073.

Basic Wildlife Rehabilitation, IAB, International Wildlife Rehabilitation Council, Suisun, California. 707/864-1761.

Introduction to Wildlife Rehabilitation, National Wildlife Rehabilitators Association, Carpenter Nature Center, Hastings, Minnesota. 612/259-4086.

Wild Animal Care and Rehabilitation, The Kalamazoo Nature Center, Kalamazoo, Michigan. 616/381-2557.

Wildlife Care and Rehabilitation, Brukner Nature Center, Troy, Ohio. 513/698-6493.

Wildlife Rescue, Inc, Austin, Texas. 713/472-WILD.

APPENDIX B

FIRST AID

If you have decided that the animal needs your care, be calm and deliberate. A deep breath helps. You will make fewer mistakes, and the animal will react positively to your calm.

First make sure that you have everything you are going to need. You can't put a rescue on hold while you go get something you have forgotten. Carry some simple items in your car and your work can begin right away.

ITEMS FOR YOUR CAR

- a strong, covered, ventilated container, heavy cardboard or plastic (this protects you and comforts and contains the animal)

- blanket, towels

- thick gloves for your protection

- a lightweight shovel (often better than hands for lifting an injured animal into container or to the side of the road—an injured creature may bite or carry parasites)

- wire cutters and scissors for traps, fences, fishing line, and so forth

HOME FIRST AID KIT

These items compose a useful home first aid kit for emergency situations.

- a suitable cage or container, cardboard box, plastic box (make sure there are air holes)
- Betadine, Clinidine, Nolvasan, or similar antiseptic wash (do not use hydrogen peroxide as it spreads bacteria into healthy tissue)
- triple antibiotic ointment, germicidal soap, petroleum jelly
- a dehydrating solution such as Pedialyte (any supermarket in baby section), Lactated Ringers (veterinarian supply), or you can make your own with:

    | 1 quart warm water | 1 cup warm water |
    | 3 Tablespoons sugar | 3/4 Tablespoon sugar |
    | 1 teaspoon salt | 1/4 teaspoon salt |

- Kaopectate or Pepto Bismol
- flea and tick water-based (safe for kittens) liquid spray containing pyrethrins (powders can be inhaled and damage eyes of birds and small mammals)

- syringes, eyedropper
- tweezers
- bandages, gauze and cotton, and tape, adhesive, masking or nonstick
- towels, soft cloths, blankets (no ragged edges, loops, holes)
- paper towels
- rubber gloves
- heavy, protective gloves, like fireplace or welders gloves
- can of puppy or kitten milk replacer, applesauce, baby rice cereal

TELEPHONE NUMBERS

TELEPHONE NUMBERS

NOTES

NOTES

NOTES

NOTES

Other Titles in the Same Series by Book Faith India

First Aid For Wildlife	— Irene Ruth
I Found A Baby Squirrel, What Do I do?	— Dale Carlson
I Found A Baby Bird, What Do I Do?	— Dale Carlson
I Found A Baby Rabbit, What Do I Do?	— Dale Carlson
I Have A Friend Who Is Deaf	— Hannah Carlson & Dale Carlson
I Have A Friend Who Is Blind	— Hannah Carlson & Dale Carlson
I Have A Friend With Mental Illness	— Hannah Carlson & Dale Carlson

---

For catalog & more information, write to:
PILGRIMS BOOK HOUSE
P. O. Box 3872, Thamel
Kathmandu, Nepal
Tel : 977-1-424942, 425919
Fax : 977-1-424943
E-mail : pilgrims@wlink.com.np
Website : www.pilgrimsbooks.com